Albert Pujols

Joanne Mattern

P.O. Box 196
Hockessin, Delaware 19707
Visit us on the web: www.mitchelllane.com
Comments? email us: mitchelllane@mitchelllane.com

08-4-23
WAE #1795

Mitchell Lane PUBLISHERS

Printing   1   2   3   4   5   6   7   8   9

A Robbie Reader
Contemporary Biography/Science Biography

Albert Einstein	**Albert Pujols**	Alex Rodriguez
Aly and AJ	Amanda Bynes	Brittany Murphy
Charles Schulz	Dakota Fanning	Dale Earnhardt Jr.
Donovan McNabb	Drake Bell & Josh Peck	Dr. Seuss
Dylan & Cole Sprouse	Henry Ford	Hilary Duff
Jamie Lynn Spears	Jessie McCartney	Johnny Gruelle
LeBron James	Mandy Moore	Mia Hamm
Miley Cyrus	Philo T. Farnsworth	Raven Symone
Robert Goddard	Shaquille O'Neal	The Story of Harley-Davidson
Syd Hoff	Tiki Barber	Thomas Edison
Tony Hawk		

Library of Congress Cataloging-in-Publication Data
Mattern, Joanne, 1963–
     Albert Pujols / by Joanne Mattern.
          p. cm. — (A Robbie reader)
     Includes bibliographical references and index.
     ISBN-13: 978-1-58415-596-6 (lib. bdg.)
     1. Pujols, Albert, 1980– —Juvenile literature. 2. Baseball players—Dominican Republic—Biography—Juvenile literature. 3. St. Louis Cardinals (Baseball team)—Juvenile literature. I. Title.
GV865.P85M38 2008
796.357092—dc22
                                                                                    2007023478

ABOUT THE AUTHOR: Joanne Mattern is the author of more than 200 nonfiction books for children. Along with biographies, she has written extensively about animals, nature, history, sports, and foreign cultures. She wrote *Brian McBride, Peyton Manning, Miguel Tejada,* and *Tiki Barber* for Mitchell Lane Publishers. She lives near New York City with her husband and four children.

PHOTO CREDITS: Cover—Tony Firriolo/MLB Photos via Getty Images; p. 4—Diamond Images/Getty Images; p. 6—David Durochik/MLB Photos via Getty Images; p. 7—AP Photo; p. 8—Jamie Squire/Getty Images; p. 12—*Sports Monthly;* p. 14—Scott Rovak/AFP/Getty Images; p. 17—Rob Tringali/Sportschrome/Getty Images; pp. 18, 20—AP Photo/James A. Finley; p. 22—AP Photo/Harry Cabluck; pp. 23, 24—AP Photo/Tom Gannam; p. 26—Jed Jacobsohn/Getty Images; p. 27—Frank Orris/WireImage.

TABLE OF CONTENTS

Like most major league players, Albert Pujols started out in the minors. Among other teams, he played for the Potomac Cannons, a minor-league team in Virginia.

Waiting for His Chance

Nineteen-year-old Albert Pujols (POO-hohls) was nervous. He had wanted to be a baseball player all his life. Now he might get his chance. He might be picked in Major **League** (LEEG) Baseball's draft.

Every year, baseball teams take turns choosing new players in the draft. The best players are usually picked early. Teams offer these players a lot of money to sign.

Round after round of the draft went by. No one picked Pujols. He knew he was a good player. Why didn't any team want him?

Finally, in the thirteenth round of the draft, the St. Louis Cardinals picked Pujols to be on their team. They offered him only $10,000 to

Pujols throws the ball during a game between the St. Louis Cardinals and the Chicago Cubs in 2001. He played in the minor leagues for only two years before he was called up to the majors.

Pujols wasn't sure if he would ever achieve his dream of playing major league baseball, but he held out for a fair deal before signing with the Cardinals.

sign with them. That was a lot less money than other players had received.

Pujols was disappointed—and mad. He told the Cardinals, "No, thank you."

The Cardinals did not forget about Pujols. They talked to him again and offered him $60,000 to sign with the team. This time, Pujols said yes. He was on his way to the major leagues!

7

During the off-season, Pujols returned home to play for the Dominican Republic in the World Baseball Classic.

Getting Noticed

Jose Alberto Pujols was born on January 16, 1980. His birthplace, Santo Domingo, is the capital of the Dominican Republic, a country on an island in the Caribbean Sea.

Alberto's parents divorced when he was very little. He never saw his mother again. His father, Bienvenido Pujols, was a **professional** (proh-FEH-shuh-nul) baseball pitcher in the Dominican Republic. He spent most of his time playing baseball. Alberto's father was his hero. He went to see his father's games whenever he could.

Although Alberto loved his father, he knew Bienvenido had a big problem. Alberto's father was an **alcoholic**. When he was an adult, Alberto recalled how hard it was when his father drank too much. "I was nine or ten years old, and I used to have to drag him home after his softball games. Every night I did it, I kept thinking to myself, 'I can never do this to my son when I grow up.' There's no way a kid should have to go through that."

Alberto lived with his grandmother and other family members. They were very poor. There was no money to buy gloves, bats, or balls for Alberto to play with. Instead, he and his friends used sticks for bats. They rolled up socks or used pieces of fruit for balls. They made gloves from cardboard milk cartons.

The family wanted a better life than they could have in the Dominican Republic. When Alberto was sixteen years old, he moved to America with his father and grandmother. They settled in the small city of Independence, Missouri.

It took a while for Alberto to get used to life in the United States. The biggest challenge was that he spoke only Spanish. When he entered Fort Osage High School, he worked hard to learn English. He also started calling himself by the American version of his name: Albert. "It was tough the first year," he later recalled. "I was shy. I knew that I needed English to communicate. So I worked hard at it, just like baseball."

Playing baseball on his high school team helped Albert fit in and make friends. He played shortstop and soon became Fort Osage's star player. In his first season, Albert's **batting average** was better than .500. He hit 11 home runs that year. One home run was especially powerful. He hit the ball 450 feet, and it landed on top of an air conditioning unit on the school's roof! Clearly, Albert was a baseball player to watch.

It did not take long for major league baseball **scouts** to hear about Albert. They came to his games and watched him lead the team to the state **championship** (CHAM-pee-un-ship).

College scouts were looking at Albert too. Albert knew that playing in college would give

Baseball helped Albert feel accepted after he moved to the United States as a teenager. He soon led Fort Osage High School to the state championships.

him more experience (ex-PEER-ee-uns) and better skills. In 1998, eighteen-year-old Albert enrolled at Maple Woods Community College in Kansas City, Missouri.

Most college players used aluminum bats because they were lighter than wooden bats. This made it easier to hit the ball. However, Albert used only wooden bats because aluminum bats weren't allowed in the major leagues. He showed up at the first day of practice swinging his wooden bat. He hit several home runs that traveled much farther than anything hit by the other players.

Albert's first season with Maple Woods got off to a great start. In his first game, he smashed a grand slam home run. Then, in the field, he turned an **unassisted** triple play! Albert got three men out all by himself. That is one of the hardest things to do in baseball.

Scouts from the St. Louis Cardinals told the team to pick Albert during the 1999 draft. The Cardinals waited until the thirteenth round of the draft to pick him. Then they offered him only $10,000 to sign. Albert said no.

"I was disappointed," he said. "I thought maybe I should quit baseball." Albert didn't quit. At the end of the summer, the Cardinals offered him $60,000. This time, he said yes.

Cardinals fans got a huge treat when Pujols stepped up to bat for the very first time in Busch Stadium in St. Louis on April 9, 2001. The rookie slammed a two-run home run!

Into the Majors

Albert's professional life was looking great. His personal life was going well too. In 1998, he met a woman named Deidre at a dance club in Kansas City. Albert and Dee-Dee liked each other right away. Dee-Dee had a baby daughter, named Isabella, who had been born with Down syndrome. Children with Down syndrome develop more slowly than other children. They need a lot of extra help to succeed in life. Dee-Dee worried that Albert would not want to spend time with Isabella. She was wrong. Albert loved Dee-Dee, and he loved Isabella, too. On January 1, 2000, Albert and Dee-Dee got married. Albert adopted Isabella as his own daughter.

After the Cardinals signed Albert, he played third base for a minor-league team called the Peoria Chiefs. He made only $126 a week! That was barely enough for him and his family to live on. "We were truly living on love," Dee-Dee said. "We ate a lot of mac and cheese in those days." Albert also worked as a waiter to make more money.

Albert was serious about baseball. Instead of partying with his teammates, he would talk to the coaches. At the end of the summer season, he had a .314 batting average, 19 home runs, and 96 **RBIs**. He quickly moved up to better minor-league teams. He usually played third base, but sometimes he played in the outfield.

In 2001, Pujols went to the Cardinals' spring training camp. He played so well there that when one of the Cardinals got hurt, the team chose Pujols to take his place. He had made it to the major leagues!

Albert and Dee-Dee had another reason to celebrate. In 2001, she gave birth to their son, Albert, Jr. They call the boy AJ.

Albert kisses his son, AJ, as his wife, Dee-Dee, looks on. AJ was born the same year that Albert was called up to the majors.

On April 9, 2001, Pujols played left field in the opening-day game at the Cardinals' Busch Stadium. When he got to the plate, he hit a home run. Pujols was the first Cardinals' **rookie** since 1954 to hit a home run in a home opener.

Many people were surprised at his success, but Pujols was not. "When you work hard, you can't be surprised," he said. "When you work hard, you get your goals."

On November 12, 2001, Albert was named the National League Rookie of the Year. His first season was amazing and included a record-setting 130 RBIs.

Better and Better

Pujols had a terrific first season with the Cardinals. He played in the All-Star Game and was voted the National League Rookie of the Year. His second season was great too. He became the first player in baseball history to have better than a .300 average, with more than 30 home runs, 100 runs scored, and 100 RBIs, all in the same year. Pujols played many different positions and often filled in for injured players. "It isn't important where I play, as long as I'm in the lineup," he told *Sporting News* in 2001.

In 2003, Pujols batted an amazing .359 and hit safely in 30 straight games. At the end of that year, he signed a seven-year deal that would pay him $100 million. Despite the money, he and his family lived simply. They had a large house, but it was not a mansion. Instead, Pujols used his money to help others. He and Dee-Dee started the Pujols Family Foundation. The foundation helps people with Down syndrome and poor families in the Dominican Republic.

In 2004, Pujols was named the Cardinals starting first baseman. That year, the Cardinals

DEIDRE PUJOLS

Albert and Dee-Dee Pujols talk to the media about their Pujols Family Foundation. The foundation helps charities in the United States and the Dominican Republic that aid poor children and children with Down syndrome.

beat the Los Angeles Dodgers in the **playoffs**. Next they faced the Houston Astros in the National League Championship Series. It took seven games, but the Cardinals won. Now they were in the World Series!

The Cardinals were no match for the Boston Red Sox. Boston swept St. Louis in four games to win the championship.

The Cardinals came back strong in 2005. Pujols hit 41 home runs and had 117 RBIs. He ended the season with a .331 batting average, the second best in the National League. Although the Cardinals easily made it to the league championships, they struggled against the Houston Astros. Pujols did his best to lead his team to victory. In game five, the Cardinals were losing by two runs in the top of the ninth inning. Then Pujols hit an awesome three-run homer to win the game 5-4. "It's the biggest hit I've ever seen," said teammate Chris Carpenter. However, the Astros went on to win the pennant and then the World Series.

Even though the Cardinals did not make it to the World Series that year, Pujols had other

In 2005, the Cardinals faced the Houston Astros in the National League Championship Series. Albert blasted a three-run homer in the ninth inning of game five. Despite that game-winning hit, the Cardinals lost the series to the Astros.

Pujols holds his daughter, Sophia, during an interview in June 2006. He is devoted to baseball, but his number-one love is his family.

reasons to celebrate. He was named the National League MVP. Even more exciting, on November 5, 2005, Dee-Dee gave birth to their daughter, Sophia.

As usual, Pujols worked hard on his game during the off-season. He was determined that the Cardinals would win it all in 2006. "I don't think about setting records," he told a reporter. "I'm trying to get my baseball team into the World Series and to win it. That's the only record I want."

Pujols is matched with honorary first baseman Brendan Hodges for the Down Syndrome Association Starting Lineup event. Albert's daughter, Isabella, has Down syndrome, and Albert has dedicated himself to helping others with this condition. On September 3, 2006, he got the whole Cardinals team involved. Each Cardinals player was matched with a child with Down syndrome when they took the field that day.

Superstar!

In 2006, the Cardinals again made it to the National League Championship Series. They defeated the New York Mets in seven games and went on to face the Detroit Tigers in the World Series.

Although Pujols did not hit very much during the series, the Cardinals beat the Tigers in just five games. At last, Pujols was a member of a championship team!

Baseball is important to Pujols, but his religious faith and his family are even more important. He also enjoys helping others. The Pujols Family Foundation has given millions of dollars to help people with Down syndrome and people living in poverty. On May 5, 2007,

In 2006, the Cardinals finally won the World Series. Albert and his son, AJ, were thrilled to hold the World Series trophy during the team's celebration after the final game.

Albert Pujols is not only a power hitter, he is also a great fielder. In 2006, he won a Gold Glove Award for fielding excellence. St. Louis third baseman Scott Rolen (right) was also a Gold Glove winner that year.

the foundation donated money to start a **vocational** school in the Dominican Republic.

February 7, 2007, marked another milestone in Albert's life. On that day, he became a United States **citizen**. Pujols was proud to learn he had a perfect score on the written citizenship test!

Albert Pujols is on top of his game, but he does not take anything for granted. "One of the mistakes a lot of young players make is that once they get to the big leagues, they think, 'That's it,' and they don't work that hard. But once you're here, you have to work extra hard to get better. I'm still working hard every day."

It's likely that Pujols still has many terrific years ahead of him. He is a power hitter, a team player, and a champion, both on and off the field.

BATTING STATISTICS

Year	Team	G	AB	R	H	2B	3B	HR	RBI	AVG
2001	SLC	161	590	112	194	47	4	37	130	.329
2002	SLC	157	590	118	185	40	2	34	127	.314
2003	SLC	157	591	137	212	51	1	43	124	.359
2004	SLC	154	592	133	196	51	2	46	123	.331
2005	SLC	161	591	129	195	38	2	41	117	.330
2006	SLC	143	535	119	177	33	1	49	137	.331
*2007	SLC	75	275	44	82	15	0	16	48	.298
*Totals		1008	3764	792	1241	275	12	266	806	.330

*Statistics as of June 27, 2007.

1980 Jose Alberto Pujols is born in Santo Domingo, Dominican Republic, on January 16.

1996 Alberto and his family move to Independence, Missouri; Alberto begins playing baseball for Fort Osage High School and using the name Albert.

1998 He meets Deidre (Dee-Dee), graduates from high school, and enrolls in Maple Woods Community College.

1999 Pujols is chosen by the St. Louis Cardinals in the thirteenth round of the draft but turns down their signing offer of $10,000; when they increase their offer to $60,000, he accepts.

2000 Albert marries Dee-Dee on January 1; he plays for several St. Louis Cardinals minor-league teams.

2001 Pujols joins the Cardinals for spring training and is signed to the starting lineup; son AJ is born; Albert is named National League Rookie of the Year.

2003 After another spectacular season, he signs a 7-year, $100-million contract with the Cardinals.

2004 He leads the National League in runs scored with 133; the Cardinals play in the World Series but lose to the Boston Red Sox.

2005 Pujols is named National League MVP; he and Dee-Dee start the Pujols Family Foundation; their daughter Sophia is born on November 5.

2006 The Cardinals win the World Series; Pujols hits a career-high 49 home runs; he wins his first Gold Glove Award. He opens a restaurant in Missouri called Pujols 5.

2007 Pujols becomes a U.S. citizen on February 7. His foundation donates $65,000 to build a vocational school in the Dominican Republic.

FIND OUT MORE

Books

Fischer, David. *Albert Pujols*. Chanhassen, Minnesota: The Child's World, 2007.

Horn, Geoffrey M. *Albert Pujols*. Milwaukee, Wisconsin: Gareth Stevens Publishing, 2006.

Savage, Jeff. *Albert Pujols*. Minneapolis: Lerner Publications Company, 2007.

Works Consulted

Burwell, Bryan. "Are Cards Fans Not Getting the Message?" *St. Louis Post-Dispatch*, May 6, 2007.

Hummel, Rick. "Phat Albert." *Sports Illustrated for Kids*, June 2003, Volume 15, Issue 6, p. 36.

Northrup, Michael. "The King of Swing." *Sports Illustrated for Kids*, June 2004, Volume 16, Issue 6, pp. 22–28.

Pujols, Albert. "My Goal Was Just to Make the Team." *Sporting News*, July 9, 2001, Volume 225, Issue 28, p. 16.

Strauss, Joe. "Albert Pujols: Baseball's Most Complete Hitter." *Baseball Digest,* August 2005, Volume 64, Issue 6, pp. 50–53.

Web Sites

ESPN.com: Albert Pujols
http://sports.espn.go.com/mlb/players/profile?player Id=4574

JockBio: Albert Pujols Biography
http://www.jockbio.com/Bios/Pujols/Pujols_bio.html

Pujols Family Foundation
http://www.pujolsfamilyfoundation.org

SI.com: Albert Pujols Player Page
http://sportsillustrated.cnn.com/baseball/mlb/players/6619

GLOSSARY

alcoholic (al-kuh-HALL-ik)—a person who has a disease that causes him or her to abuse alcohol.

batting average (BAA-ting AV-ridj)—the number of hits a baseball player gets per times at bat.

championship (CHAM-pee-un-ship)—a final game or series of games that decides which team is the winner of the season.

citizen (SIH-tuh-zun)—someone who was born in a country or who has moved there and passes a test to stay permanently.

league (LEEG)—a group of teams that play against one another.

playoffs (PLAY-offs)—games to determine which teams will play for the championship.

professional (proh-FEH-shuh-nul)—someone who is paid to do a job.

RBIs—runs batted in; the number of players who score as a result of a hit.

rookie (RUH-kee)—a player in his or her first professional season.

scout (SKOWT)—someone who looks for new players for a team.

unassisted (un-uh-SIS-ted)—without help.

vocational (voh-KAY-shun-nul)—something that teaches skills useful for work.

INDEX